Dark Web

Demystified

Into the Power of Anonymity

Adarsh Nair

Greeshma M R

ISBN-13: 9798646848452

Imprint: Independently Published

DEDICATION

To all Builders, Breakers, and Defenders who keep the
cyberspace strong and safe.

Table of Contents

ACKNOWLEDGMENT

Lockdown time was never a "less happening" one.
To our family, without whose support this book
would not have been possible, who helped us steer
through the challenges of being new parents.
To the latest member of the family, Samanyu, our son.

INTRODUCTION

I nternet technology has made surveillance widespread and a lot simpler to execute, while at the same time making personal privacy more challenging to protect. The extensive processing of personal data has increased public consciousness of data privacy violations. There are many initiatives to supply Privacy Enhancing Technologies (PETs) to protect customers' data privacy. Among them, a very well-known PET is The Onion Router (Tor), which supplies users with Internet anonymity.

Tor is supported by a team of volunteers that donate their resources to maintain the service's accessibility and quality. However, Tor volunteers can find themselves in a tough place occasionally since the Tor community is frequently tracked by law enforcement agencies, making this PET community distinct from any other open-source initiatives.

Onion routing is a method of making communication over the Internet anonymously. Messages are encapsulated within an onion structure in layers of protection. Encoded data is distributed through a network node sequence named onion routers; each node 'peels' a single layer, finding the next destination of the data. The message arrives at its destination as soon as the last layer is decrypted. The sender stays anonymous because every intermediary knows the positioning of the preceding and succeeding nodes.

The Web we know comprises of the Surface Web, the Deep Web, and the Dark Web.

Surface Web is what we come across daily, the internet information we consume using browsers. It comprises of contents that appear as a result of our search query (say, on the n number of Google result pages).

The Deep Web includes email communications, chats, personal information on social networking platforms, electronic bank account statements, Electronic Health Records (EHRs) and other resources that can be viewed via the regular Internet but is not identified or indexed by regular search engines such as Google, Yahoo, Bing, etc.

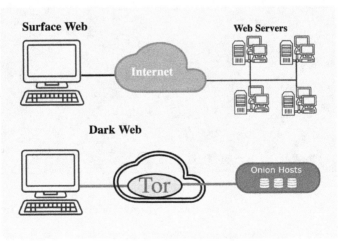

Fig: Surface Web vs Dark Web

The Dark Web is the darkest portion of the Internet. In other words, it is the tiny and deeper part of the Deep Web in which the contents are deliberately obscured to maintain secrecy and privacy. Dark Web pages are not indexed by search engines and remain anonymous. When we want to see particular objects in a dark room, we need the help of a light source. Similarly, we need the aid of specific browsers like Tor to access pages on the Dark Web.

The terms Dark Web and Deep Web are often used interchangeably and incorrectly too. The Deep Web includes all the pages which do not show up when you run a web search. The pages which require login such as Internet banking accounts are part of the Deep Web. The Dark Web also forms a part of the Deep Web, which cannot be accessed through regular web browsers like Internet Explorer, Chrome, Firefox, etc.

Peer-to-peer (p2p) network is a group of computers, each of which serves as both client and server so that each of them can share resources directly with every other computer on the network. Every computer can access all of the others, but access could be restricted to specific files that the owner of the machine wants to make accessible. Tor implements p2p communication architecture.

1 WORLD WIDE WEB (WWW)

The Web is a widely used term for the World Wide Web, a subset of the Internet that is composed of sites that can be viewed by an Internet browser client. Most people believe that the Web is just like the Internet, hence use both terms interchangeably. Based on the content accessed, the Web can be divided into three layers: **Surface Web**, **Deep Web**, and **Dark Web**.

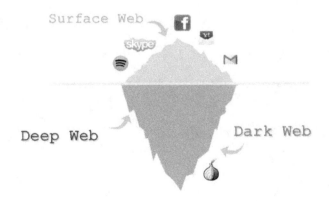

1. Surface Web

Surface Web is also called the Visible Web or Clear Web or Indexable Web. It is what we all know and sees regularly. It is the part of the World Wide Web that is freely available to the general public and searchable using conventional search engines.

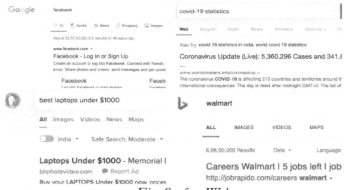

Fig: Surface Web

It means that the search engines are indexing the Surface Web pages, and the users will get the details as part of the search results. Interestingly, it forms only about 4% of the information available on the Internet. You may navigate this list of web pages through any search engine.

The Surface Web is available via search engines like Google, Bing, Yahoo, etc. Search engines crawl and index the pages to be found on the Internet to ensure it is accessible to users.

To summarize, the Surface Web is the part of the web that we are all aware of and use regularly! However, as we mentioned before, this is merely 4 percent of the internet! Know what represents the 96 percent in the subsequent sections.

2. Deep Web

Deep Web or Invisible Web are components of the World Wide Web, the contents of which are not indexed by conventional search engines. These contents are hidden behind HTTP forms. The non-indexing of Deep Web pages is for various reasons. It may be proprietary, or a commercial resource, which can only be accessed by consumers who have paid the fee, or it may be some critical and confidential content containing Personally Identifiable Information (PII), Protected Health Information (PHI), etc. which is protected by various compliance regulations or maybe some contents are secured by authentication and authorization. They include webmail, online banking, and other services that users must pay for and hence, are protected using a payment gateway. For entry to the public web page using a direct URL, additional authentication is required.

Fig: Authenticated Page

The information saved on the Deep Web includes military information, individual information, financial documents, instructional databases, valid dossiers, medical records, social networking profile information, and government and scientific documents. These can be accessed if a person gets the login or consent credentials to do so.

3. Dark Web

The Dark Web consists of web resources or web pages that are also part of the World Wide Web. Leveraged on overlay networks, they require specific software or authorization to access (like how we need a torch to see in the dark). The Dark Net can be in the form of small peer-to-peer networks or large conventional networks such as Tor, Freenet, etc., run by public institutions or individuals. Like Deep Web, the Dark Web is also the area of the Internet that is not indexed by search engines.

Fig: Dark Web

The Dark Web is frequently viewed as a forum for obscure and illegal activities due to its anonymity. The websites on the Dark Web have a unique URL that ends with an *onion* extension. [*Websitename*].*onion* domains are not indexed by standard search engines, and you can only navigate the Dark Web using special tools.

The users can access the Dark Web using specialized software and an anonymizing browser (Tor is the most popular one). Tor is often called an Onion browser, which comprises of many layers. It enables a user to be anonymous, i.e., it neither traces the user's IP address/location nor records any detail.

The user's web page requests are sent through a chain of proxy servers, from source to destination, which renders the IP address untraceable and unidentifiable. The Tor system operates by encrypting/decrypting content in every message, at each point, which makes it hard and nearly impossible to monitor their point of incident or origin.

2 CRYPTOGRAPHY

C ryptography is the method of preserving the secrecy of information and communication by the use of codes so that it can be read and interpreted only by those for whom the information is intended. The prefix "crypt-" means "secret," and the suffix "-graphy" means "writing." Hence, Cryptography means "Secret Writing".

Encryption and Decryption are the essential components of cryptography. In today's digital world, cryptography is most frequently associated with disordering plaintext (ordinary text, often referred to as cleartext) into ciphertext (a process called encryption), then back again (known as decryption).

The word "cryptography" descended from the Greek word kryptos. The root of cryptography is typically dated with the Egyptian hieroglyphics tradition from around 2000 B.C., which was the formal writing system used in Ancient Egypt. These consisted of complex pictograms whose complete significance was understood only to a few of the elite.

Julius Caesar (100 B.C. to 44 B.C.), was the first who recorded the use of a modern cipher. For this purpose, he developed a scheme in which the Roman alphabet replaced each character in his messages with a character three positions ahead of it. For example,

ABCDEF... can be written as
CDEFG...

Recently cryptography has become a battleground with some of the greatest mathematicians and computer scientists in the world. The ability to store and transmit confidential information in a secure manner has given a broader acceptance to cryptographic techniques across the globe.

The classical cryptography uses Substitution or Transposition techniques. The Transposition ciphers rearrange the order of letters in a message (e.g., 'hello world' becomes 'ehlol owrdl' in a trivially easy rearrangement scheme), and substitution ciphers systematically substitute letters or groups of letters with other letters or groups of letters (e.g., 'fly at once' becomes

'gmz bu podf' by replacing each letter with the next letter).
The ancient Greeks used **scytale**, which is a tool used to
perform a transposition cipher.

Fig: Scytale

In Caesar cipher (an early substitution cipher), each
letter in the plaintext was replaced by a letter at a fixed
number of positions further down the alphabet. Suetonius
(a Roman Historian) states that Julius Caesar used it to
interact with his troops, with a change of three.

One of the earliest known substitution methods is the
Kamasutra cipher, described in Vatsyayana's Kamasutra in
around 400 B. C., which recommends women to study 64
arts, among which number 44 on the list is *Mlecchita
Vikalpa* (the art of secret writing). It teaches women how

to hide secret messages from prying eyes. A sug   u

strategy involves randomly pairing letters of the alphabet and then substituting each letter in the original message with its partner. For example, if letters *a* and *b* are paired, *a* will be used instead of *b*, and *b* is replaced with *a* in the text.

Steganography is a method of hiding only the presence of a message to keep it confidential. An example, from the time of Herodotus (an ancient Greek Historian), was a message tattooed on the shaved head of a slave and concealed under the recovered hair. More recent steganography examples include the use of invisible ink, microdots, and digital watermarks to cover details.

The main components in a cryptographic system are:

- **Plain Text**: An intelligible data with proper meaning.
- **Cipher Text**: An unintelligible data that is hard to interpret.
- **Encryption**: Process of converting plaintext to ciphertext.
- **Decryption**: Process of converting ciphertext to plaintext.
- **Cryptographic Algorithm**: Set of clear instructions to Encrypt or Decrypt the data.
- **Cryptographic Keys**: Keys used for encryption or decryption process.

In modern cryptography, there are broadly two classifications - Symmetric Key Cryptography and Asymmetric Key Cryptography.

1. Symmetric Key Cryptography

It is also called Private Key Cryptography or Secret Key Cryptography. Here, the same key is used for both encryption and decryption, which is considered a more secure and efficient method for sharing data even in large quantities.

The encrypted message can be decrypted only by the same key, which is used for encryption. Hence, the Secret Key is also required to be shared with the recipient. This is one of the challenges in Symmetric Cryptography - how to share the keys securely?

Advanced Encryption Standards (AES), Data Encryption Standard (DES), Rivest Cipher 5 (RC5), etc. are a few examples of Symmetric Cryptographic implementations.

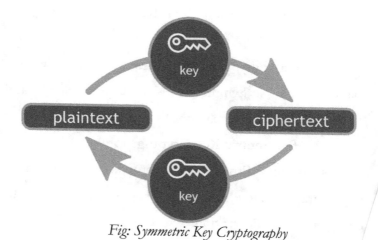

Fig: Symmetric Key Cryptography

2. Asymmetric Key Cryptography

It is also known as Public Key Cryptography. Every participant in the Asymmetric Cryptographic system should have a key pair; Public Key and Private Key. The Public Key is accessible to all participants, and the Private Key is only known to the owner.

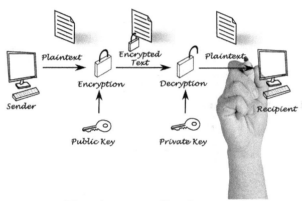

Fig: Asymmetric Key Cryptography

A message which is encrypted using public key can be decrypted only using its corresponding private key, which ensures the secrecy or confidentiality of the message. Similarly, the message encrypted using private key can be decrypted only by its public key, which provides the authenticity of the message. RSA (Rivest–Shamir–Adleman), ElGamal, etc. are a few examples.

Generally, a combination of symmetric and asymmetric cryptographic methods is used. The actual encryption of data is done by using symmetric cryptography, and the secret key is shared with the recipient using asymmetric cryptography. That means, the generated secret key is encrypted using the recipient's public key so that the actual key can be retrieved only using the corresponding private key which belongs to the recipient.

Diffie-Hellman Key Exchange Algorithm

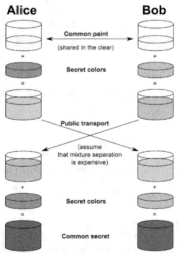

Fig: Illustration - Diffie-Hellman Key Exchange Algorithm

It is the first key exchange algorithm that helps for the secure exchange of cryptographic keys over a public communication channel. Here, rather than sharing the keys, the keys are derived jointly by both communicating parties.

As illustrated in the above figure, the sender and receiver choose their private value (Secret Color) and public value (Common Paint). By performing some mathematical calculations on their public and private values, they generate new value and share with each other. Each party does another set of calculations and derive the key, which is the same for both parties. Hence, the sender and receiver share the secret key among each other without sharing the exact key as such.

Fig: SHA Types

Hashing

Hashing is the process of converting or transforming variable-length characters into a fixed-length string, which is irreversible. That means from the fixed-length output, none can interpret the original text.

This property is called One Way hashing. The fixed-length product is called Message Digest or Hash. MD-5 (Message Digest-5), SHA-1 (Secure Hash Algorithms-1), SHA-2, SHA-3, etc. are a few examples of hashing algorithms.

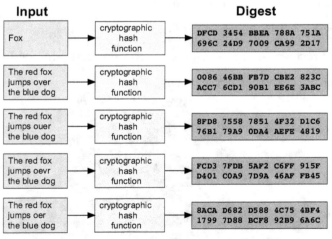

Fig: Hashing Samples

Hashing methods are used to verify the integrity of a message. The hash value of a message using the same algorithm is always the same. Thus, if there is any alteration that happened in the message, the hash value would be a different one.

Even a single space will make a significant change in the hash value. Digital Signatures, which are used to verify the authenticity in digital space, is another application of hashing.

3 ONION ROUTING

Onion Routing was created by the United States Naval Research Laboratory personnel, Mathematician Paul Syverson and Computer Scientists Michael G. Reed and David Goldschlag, in the mid-1990s to encrypt U.S. intelligence communications online. DARPA (Defense Advanced Research Projects Agency) further developed the Onion Routing in 1997.

Tor is an implementation of the Onion Routing Protocol, and Tor stands for The Onion Router. It was created by Paul Syverson and Computer Scientists Roger Dingledine and Nick Mathewson and released on 20 September 2002.

In 2004, the Naval Research Laboratory published the Tor code under a free license. The Tor Project Inc. is a non-profit organization that manages Tor and is responsible for its production.

The soul of Dark Web, Onion Routing, is an anonymous communication method on a computer network. Each device linked to the Onion network recognizes itself as a node. Messages are continuously encrypted and then transmitted across a set of network nodes called Onion Routers.

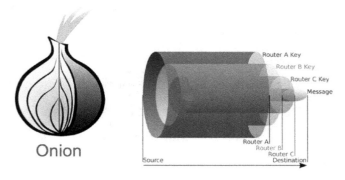

Fig: Onion Structure

Messages are stored in cells and unwrapped at each node or onion router with a symmetric key. The onion nodes drop the encrypted layer to expose the routing instructions and send the message to the next router where this process will be replicated until it reaches the destination. It is just like peeling an onion!

In the figure above, a message is encrypted with the keys of different nodes (which are part of the particular communication) and sent from a source. One layer is peeled off from outside to inside at each node, analogous to the peeling of onion and hence the term. The encrypted message is called onion.

Tor is an anonymizing software, which anonymizes applications like instant messaging, secure shell, web browsing, etc.

Tor clients select a route through the system and construct a circuit, where every node from the trail knows its predecessor and successor, but no other nodes in the circuit.

Traffic flows down the path through fixed-sized cells, which will be unwrapped by a symmetric key at every node (such as onion layers) and transmitted downstream.

We often praise Tor for privacy and the anonymity it supplies to those who wish to conceal activities, who are terrified of being detained by the government, and those who possess sensitive data, which can be misused or removed by hackers.

Tor faces criticism because it functions as a medium for distinct illegal actions like data breaching, drug trading, gambling, child pornography, etc. Tor can also be employed by criminals to communicate over the Internet while keeping their identity concealed, making it hard for the security agencies to track them. Though the Tor application was created by programmers for military functions, it has grown into a tool that may be helpful to all -- particularly to people who have something to conceal or may benefit from online anonymity.

Tor is used across various disciplines ranging from individuals, activists, journalists, NGOs, corporates, and law enforcement authorities. These people may also be residing in nations where they might be punished by authorities for the perspectives and ideas they discuss online.

Individuals may use Tor for politically conscious contact in chat rooms, online pages, etc. such as rape and abuse survivors, or people with illnesses as well as people who need to protect their identity and communications from surveillance, like whistle-blowers and journalists.

Journalists utilize Tor to interact more freely with reporters. They also use it to secure their sources. If a source doesn't need to be disclosed, they could communicate privately through Tor. Dissidents in oppressive cultures that are refused freedom of expression use it to stay confidential, to learn what is occurring everywhere in the world, and to reveal what they wish to tell the rest of the world. A lot of people use the Tor browser to obtain geo-restricted content, to bypass censorship and access online content.

As an example, one of Tor's most prominent users and supporters would be Edward Snowden, who disclosed documents on categorized surveillance applications in the United States. In the same way, workers can use Tor to expose government or company secrets or address actions.

Non-governmental organizations (NGOs) use Tor to encourage their staff to link to their website when they are in a foreign country, without notifying others around that they are collaborating for a different organization.

Corporates utilize Tor as a safe way of performing strategic analyses and shielding private procurement practices from eavesdroppers. Law enforcement uses Tor to access or track websites without leaving actual IP addresses in their weblogs and to maintain confidentiality during sting operations.

Using Tor itself is legal in many countries, particularly in the "western world." Due to anonymity, the program helps users in criminal activities; some people today use Tor for prohibited actions.

Having Tor saves you from a popular type of Internet monitoring known as "traffic analysis." Traffic analysis may be used to determine who is communicating through a public network. Understanding the origins and destination of your traffic on the Web helps others to trace your actions and interests. For example, an e-commerce site can use price discrimination based on your country of origin. This can also risk your career and physical health by exposing who you are and where you are.

How does traffic analysis work? The Internet data packets have two parts: a payload of data and a routing header. Payload data is anything you send, whether it's an email message, a web link, or an audio file. Even if you encrypt the content of your communications, traffic analysis always shows a great opportunity about what you're doing and, probably, what you're saying. This is because it focuses on trends that expose source, target, size, timing, and so on.

An elementary form of traffic analysis might involve intercepting messages between the sender and recipient on the network and examining patterns. These can include permitted intermediaries, such as Internet Service Providers, and also unauthorized intermediaries such as man-in-the-middle attacks. In some of the most effective forms of traffic analysis, attackers spy on different sections of the Internet and use advanced statistical tools to map the trends of communication through a wide variety of entities and individuals. Encryption can only hide the content of Internet traffic, but not patterns, and thus may not be able to help fight such attacks.

Downside of Tor

Tor is helpful but has its imperfections. Browsing with Tor may not be as anonymous as you may hope. Even the people who maintain the Tor network are always working to enhance their security, as their applications were hacked previously. Tor stated that it was not their system and network which was breached, but instead specific browsers. But although this may reassure users, this still reveals Tor isn't ideal as a standalone privacy measure.

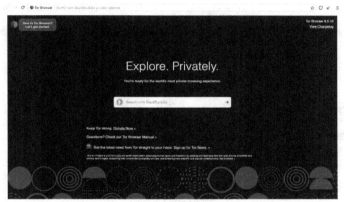

Fig: Tor Browser

The anonymity that Tor provides us may not be enough of a bonus to incite the use of the program. It is because the encryption can make your link and connection slower. Besides, carrying out online surveillance still costs time and money, which means governments cannot – and very likely do not even want to – spy on every single one of their civilians. They must concentrate on questionable behavior.

That is why many people who invest their time online for normal activities will probably not gain much from using the Tor browser.

Whether you need to use Tor depends upon what you require. Tor is free of charge, simple to use, and usually a very powerful privacy program. It provides you access to the Dark Web and contains many choices to secure your online privacy.

Anonymous websites are hosted via Tor's Onion Services. With the help of Tor, the Dark Web users and content creators roam around the Internet without any fear, keeping themselves and their real identities are hidden from law enforcement agencies.

4 WORKING OF TOR

Tor distributes the transactions to different locations on the Internet. It throws away the one that follows you and erases the 'fingerprints' regularly. Rather than following a straight route from source to destination, data packets on the Tor network follow a random path through multiple relays that hide the traces, and no observer at any stage will say where the data is coming from or where it is heading.

The nodes recognize either the successor or predecessor, with no other references. This prevents such intermediate nodes from understanding the source, destination, and meaning of the communication. Tor channels Internet traffic through an open, global, voluntary network of more than 7,000 relays to mask the identity and usage of users from those performing network monitoring or traffic analysis. Onion routing is enforced by encrypting the communication protocol stack in the application layer.

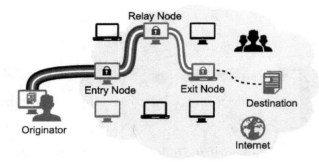

The systems that form the part of Tor communication are called nodes. There are mainly three types of nodes: Entry Node (Starting node in the circuit by which the user is connecting to the Tor network), Relay Node (Intermediary nodes which transmit the cells), and Exit Node (Last node in the circuit that connects directly to the destination). The whole communication channels are encrypted except the connection from the Exit node in the circuit to the destination.

The first phase of Tor communication is the circuit establishment. For each communication, there will be one Entry Node, one Exit Node, and N number of Relay

Nodes. The basic unit of Tor communication is Cells, which is 512 bytes in size.

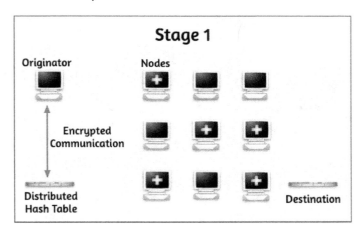

There are two types of cells: control cells (create, destroy, etc.) and relay cells (carry end to end stream data). Every node associated with the Tor network has a public-private key pair (Asymmetric Key – RSA 1024), which is used for the establishment of an encryption key. The Tor client will initiate the symmetric key generation with every node, one node at a time, using a Diffie-Hellman Key exchange algorithm.

Once the keys are established, the second phase will start. The intended message cells will be encrypted multiple times using the keys established with each node in the previous phase. The encryption will be done in the reverse order of the decryption.

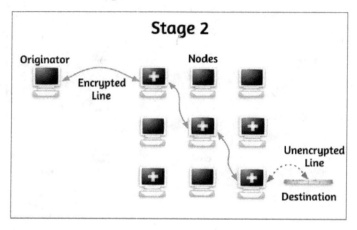

It means that the cell will be encrypted using the Exit Node's keys first, then with Relay Nodes' keys and finally with Entry Node's key. Advanced Encryption Standard (AES) symmetric cryptographic algorithm is used for the encryption and decryption process.

Tor circuit will take a random pathway, which includes several intermediary nodes that cover your tracks. At any point in time, the intermediate nodes cannot read the actual message content or the details about the originator or the recipient. They just know which Relay Node gave it data, and to which relay it should provide data to. Therefore, no single relay ever knows the entire route a data packet has taken. The circuit will be the same for the connections that happen within the same 10 minutes. Hence, it ensures the secrecy and anonymity throughout the communication process.

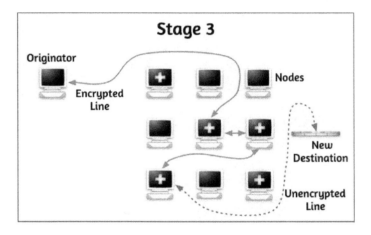

The Tor does not interact with the system files in the machine in which it is installed. It can be installed and run from a removable disk as well. This is an extremely welcomed feature because it simplifies the risk that somebody can infect your backup of the Tor browser and can discover your precise browsing data regardless of the IP address you're using.

You aren't just an individual while you're browsing, but a proxy for people who are currently utilizing your IP address node to conceal their IP address. This approach of the users is contributing to the safety and anonymity of Tor community.

5 ONION SERVICES

O nion Services, which was formerly known as Hidden Services of Tor, helps people to mask their identity (location) when providing various services like online web applications, instant chat applications, file transfers, etc. The Dark Web is one of the leading implementations of onion services, which provides secrecy and anonymity.

Onion services can only be accessed using Tor. It offers various security and privacy benefits. Few of them are:

- **Hiding Identity**: The client and server IP addresses remain hidden and are not at all used in the communication protocol.

- **End to End Authentication**: The users can be sure that the content they are viewing is coming from that original onion site. The chances of impersonation are negligible.

- **End to End Encryption**: Client to Onion host connection is encrypted.

The users can connect to the onion services using Tor's Rendezvous Points (RP) without revealing the systems' identity. The detailed steps are:

1. Setting up Introduction Points (IPs)

The onion program randomly chooses a few Relay Nodes, create circuits for them, and tells them to serve as Introduction Points (IP) by revealing their public key. The Onion Services never reveals their location to IPs and remains anonymous.

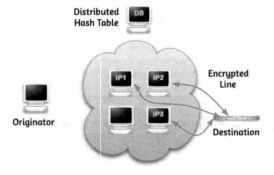

Onion Services - Step 1

2. Publishing Service Descriptors (SD)

Onion Services - Step 2

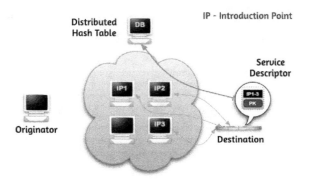

An onion service has to announce its presence on the Tor network before it can be approached by users. The onion services create a Service Descriptor, which includes the details about the introduction points along with its authentication keys, which will be encrypted by its private key. The service descriptor will be uploaded to a distributed hash table using an anonymized Tor circuit, from which the users can access it.

The descriptor will be located by customers asking ABC.onion in which ABC is a 16-character name derived from the service's public key. The version 2 onion address is base 32 of the first half of the SHA-1 hash of the service's public key. It contains a 16-character string, which has a combination of lower cap letters *a* to *z* and digits from *2* to *7*. The Dark Web address is generally known as an onion address.

Onion Services - Step 3

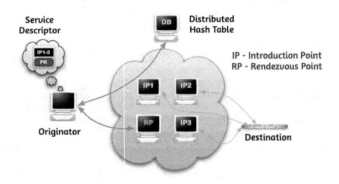

3. Client accessing Onion Services

A client who wishes to access the onion service should know about its onion address. Once the client gets the address, the connection initiation will be done by downloading the service descriptor from the distributed hash table to the client.

Then, the client gets the details about the introduction points and public key from the service descriptor and verifies the signature of the descriptor using the public key that is encoded in the onion address. This ensures the End to End authentication property since the signature is verified using the Onion Host's public key.

4. Establishing Rendezvous Points (RPs)

Onion Services - Step 4

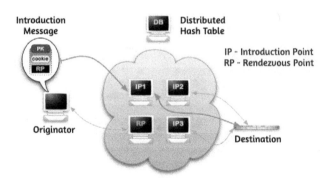

The client randomly chooses a relay, and generates a circuit to it, sending a one-time secret and instructing it to serve as a rendezvous point.

5. Client Introduction to Onion Services

As the next step, the client will create an introduction message, which is encrypted using the onion service's public key, containing the rendezvous point's address and the one-time secret. The introduction points will route this message to the onion services.

Onion Services - Step 5

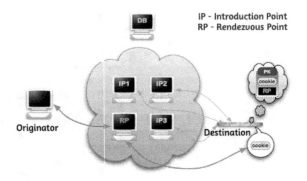

Since communication is happening through Tor circuits, the nodes' identity remains anonymous. The onion service will decrypt the message and create a circuit to the rendezvous points and send back a rendezvous message to the client through rendezvous points, which includes the one-time secret (cookie) for the connection.

6. Onion Service Connection Establishment

Onion Services - Step 6

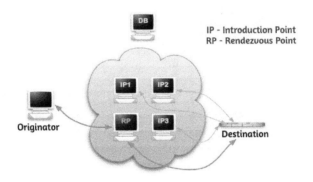

In the last step, the rendezvous point intimates the client about the successful connection, and the client/service uses the connection to the rendezvous point for communication. The rendezvous points relay the end to end encrypted communications between client and services.

The entire connection consists of six relays in which three of them are chosen by the client, and the remaining relays are selected by the onion services. Hence it provides the Hidden Identity feature.

Version 3 of onion services has some significant improvements over the previous version. The major upgrade is in terms of onion addresses. Now, the address is 56-character long, which is a combination of 56 base32 characters that correctly encodes an ed25519 public key, a checksum, and a version number.

[Example:*4acth47i6nxnvkewtm6q7ib2s4ufpo5sqbsnziobi7uti jcltosqewac.onion*]

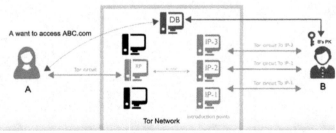

Fig: Onion Service

The other significant improvements are:

- Implemented strong crypto (replaced SHA1/DH/RSA1024 with SHA3/ed25519/curve25519)

- Directory protocol improvement with leaking less information to directory servers.
- Directory protocol has improved with smaller surfaces for targeted attacks.
- Onion address security has improved against impersonation.
- Introduction/rendezvous protocol is more extensible.
- Onion services have offline keys.
- Client authorization is advanced.

6 CRYPTOCURRENCIES

C ryptocurrency is a digital or virtual currency protected by cryptography, which makes counterfeiting or double-spending almost impossible. Also known as digital currency, it is a system that allows secure online payments to be denominated as virtual "tokens," represented by internal system ledger entries. The individual digital token coin ownership records are stored in a digital ledger or computerized database using strong cryptography to secure financial transaction record entries, monitor the production of additional digital token coin records, and verify the transfer of token coin ownership. Blockchain is the underlying technology for cryptocurrencies.

Blockchain

It is a distributed ledger technology that verifies and permanently records transactions between two parties.

Each block contains the transaction data, a hash pointer as a link to the previous block, and a timestamp. Blockchains are, by definition, fundamentally resistant to data alteration. A blockchain is typically managed for use as a distributed ledger by a peer-to-peer network.

The nodes or computers in the network collectively adhere to a protocol for validating new blocks. Only validated blocks are added to the chain. The data can't be altered retroactively in any given block without altering all subsequent blocks, which requires enormous computing power and is practically impossible.

Blockchain originally started as a record-keeping system to record the transfer of digital 'tokens' or 'coins' such as Bitcoin and other cryptocurrencies, and thus maintaining a record of digital ownership. Blockchains are safe by nature and are an example of a distributed computing system with a high tolerance for Byzantine faults.

"Blocks" are composed of digital pieces of knowledge on the blockchain. Blocks store information which differentiates them from other blocks. Just like you and I have names that distinguish us from each other, every block stores a specific code called a "hash" that helps us to tell each block apart from every other block. Hashes are cryptographic codes generated by algorithms of unique nature.

Blockchain can only be modified by consensus between network members (nodes) and can never be removed once new data is entered. This is a write-once, append-many system, making each transaction a verifiable and auditable record. Bitcoin, which is a cryptocurrency, was one of the most popular implementations of blockchain.

Cryptocurrency

Many cryptocurrencies are decentralized, blockchain-based networks — a distributed database operated by a fragmented computer network. One distinguishing characteristic of cryptocurrencies is that they are usually not distributed by any central authority, rendering them technically resistant to intervention or abuse by the government.

It is a new type of digital asset based on a network spread over a large number of computers. This decentralized structure allows them to operate beyond the influence of the central authorities and governments.

"Crypto" refers to the various encryption algorithms and cryptographic methods that safeguard these entries, such as elliptical curve cryptography, public-private key pairs, and hash functions.

Use for illicit activity, exchange rate fluctuations, etc. are some of the reasons why cryptocurrencies come under scrutiny. They were also praised for their portability, divisibility, resistance to inflation, and openness, however.

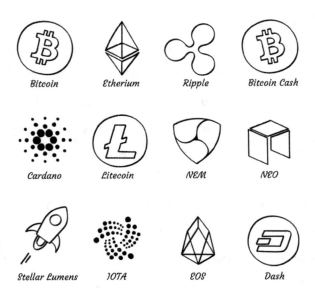

Fig: Crypocurrencies

Bitcoin, first released in 2009 as open-source software, is widely regarded as the first decentralized cryptocurrency. More than 6,000 altcoins (alternative versions of bitcoin, or other cryptocurrencies) were generated after the release of bitcoin.

Bitcoin and Digital Currencies

Bitcoin is a decentralized digital currency based on peer-to-peer bitcoin network architecture, which enables transmissions from user to user without the need for intermediaries, a central bank, or a single administrator. A blockchain establishes the authenticity of the coins for each crypto-currency.

Transactions are registered in a publicly distributed ledger called a blockchain and are cryptographically validated by network nodes. The concept was brought in while Bitcoin's pseudonymous author, Satoshi Nakamoto, presented about blockchain in the BTC white paper in 2008. Blockchain technology began this way with the Bitcoin network. Though blockchain has since seen use in several other fields, it has been developed primarily for this digital currency and, more generally, for advancing digital currency goals in some sense.

Bitcoin was made as open-source software in 2009 when its source code was made available. The mining process carried out by participating devices earns rewards in bitcoins. New bitcoins are created through mining, and the participating devices are called 'miners'. Bitcoin can be traded for other currencies and utilities. It provides lower transaction costs than conventional electronic payment systems and is regulated by a decentralized body, unlike currencies issued by the government.

Bitcoin faces criticism for its use in illegal transactions, its high consumption of energy, and market fluctuations. It has been characterized as a speculative bubble by some economists, including many Nobel laureates. No banks or governments issue or back bitcoins, nor are individual bitcoins valuable as an asset. While it is not a legal tender, Bitcoin is widely popular and has spawned hundreds of other virtual currencies collectively referred to as Altcoins.

Bitcoin tokens balances are held using both public and private "keys," which are long strings of numbers and letters connected by the mathematical encryption algorithm used to build them. The public key is like a bank account number that acts as the address that is released to the world and can be submitted by others to bitcoins. The private key can be compared to an ATM PIN and is a guarded secret used to approve transmissions.

How Bitcoin Works

Bitcoin is among the early digital currencies to use peer-to-peer technology to make instant payments simpler. The autonomous individuals and companies that own the regulating computing resources and participate in the Bitcoin network, also referred to as "miners," are driven by incentives (the creation of new bitcoin) and transaction fees paid in bitcoin. Those miners can be seen as the decentralized authority that enforces the Bitcoin network's legitimacy. In this way, Bitcoin (and any cryptocurrency created by a similar process) works differently from fiat currency; in centralized banking systems, the currency is released at a rate that matches the growth of commodities in an attempt to preserve price stability, whereas a decentralized system such as Bitcoin sets the release rate in advance and accordance with an algorithm.

Bitcoin mining is the mechanism that releases bitcoins into circulation. Mining typically involves the solving of computationally challenging puzzles to discover a new block that is added to the blockchain. Mining adds and verifies transaction records across the network, in adding to the blockchain.

Miners receive a reward in the form of a few bitcoins to add blocks to the blockchain; the reward is halved for every 210,000 blocks. When more and more bitcoins are being produced, the mining process's complexity-that is the amount of computational power involved-is growing. Mining difficulty started at 1.0 with Bitcoin debut back in 2009; it was just 1.18 at the end of the year.

As of October 2019, the mining risk reaches 12 trillion. In the past, an ordinary desktop computer was enough for the mining process. But now, to overcome the degree of difficulty, costly and sophisticated hardware such as Application-Specific Integrated Circuits (ASIC) and more advanced processing units such as Graphics Processing Units (GPUs) need to be used.

These complicated mining processors are called "mining machines." One bitcoin is divisible to eight decimal places (100 millionths of a bitcoin), and this smallest unit is called a Satoshi. If required, and if the move is agreed by the participating miners, Bitcoin could eventually be divided into even more decimals.

What's a Bitcoin Worth?

In 2017 alone, Bitcoin's price rose from just under $1,000 at the beginning of the year to nearly $19,000, finishing the year more than 1,400 percent. More recently, the asset had fallen in value and plateaued more or less, saving comparatively lower price figures for a few periods (the early portion of 2019, when prices hovered about $3,500) and significantly higher prices (June and July 2019, when prices peaked briefly at more than $13,000). At present (May 2020), it is over $9000.

Bitcoin's price depends pretty much on the scale of its mining network because the larger the network is, the more comfortable – and thus costlier – it is to produce new bitcoins. As a result, bitcoin's prices continue to increase as their production costs also grow.

The aggregate processing power of the Bitcoin mining network is known as the "hash rate," referring to the number of times the network may attempt to complete a required hashing puzzle before adding a block to the blockchain.

The following is a brief timeline of some of the most important events in blockchain and cryptocurrency in general and bitcoin in particular:

⇒ **2008**

       o   Satoshi Nakamoto publishes "Bitcoin: A Peer to Peer Electronic Cash Network," the acronym for an individual or community.

⇒ **2009**

       o   The first successful Bitcoin (BTC) transaction is between Hal Finney, a computer scientist, and the enigmatic Satoshi Nakamoto.

⇒ **2010**

- o Florida programmer Laszlo Hanycez completes the first-ever Bitcoin purchase — two Papa John's pizzas. Hanycez transferred 10,000 BTC's at the time, worth about $60. It's reportedly worth $80 million today.

- o Bitcoin's market cap reportedly reaches $1 million.

⇒ **2011**

- o 1 BTC = $1 USD, granting the US dollar parity to the crypto-currency.

- o Electronic Frontier Foundation, Wikileaks, and other organizations are starting to recognize Bitcoin as their donations.

⇒ **2012**

- o In popular television shows like The Good Wife, blockchain and cryptocurrency are listed, injecting blockchain into pop culture.

o Bitcoin Magazine founded by Vitalik Buterin, an early Bitcoin developer.

⇒ **2013**

o The market cap on the BTC reached $1 billion.

o The first time Bitcoin hit $100/BTC.

o Buterin introduces Ethereum and Smart Contracts in a whitepaper, and establishes that blockchain has other choices beyond Bitcoin (e.g., smart contracts).

⇒ **2014**

o Gaming business Zynga, Hotel D Las Vegas, and Overstock.com are all beginning to embrace Bitcoin as payment.

o The Ethereum Project is launched via crowdfunding as the first smart contract with an Initial Coin Offering (ICO) raising more than $18 million in BTC and opening up new blockchain avenues.

o R3, a consortium of more than 200 blockchain firms, is being founded to find new ways to apply blockchain in technology.

o PayPal announces integration with Bitcoin.

⇒ **2015**

o The number of merchants that support BTC is more than 100,000.

o NASDAQ begins a blockchain trial.

o Linux Foundation establishes the Hyperledger project.

⇒ **2016**

o IT giant IBM is developing a plan for cloud-based enterprise applications using a blockchain.

- o Japan's government considers blockchain and cryptocurrencies as valid.

⇒ **2017**

- o The first time Bitcoin hits $1,000/BTC.
- o The market cap for cryptocurrency crosses $150 billion.
- o JP Morgan CEO Jamie Dimon says he trusts in blockchain as a technology of the future, granting Wall Street's ledger program a vote of confidence.
- o Bitcoin hits $19,783.21/BTC to its all-time peak.
- o Dubai reveals that it will have blockchain control over its government by 2020.

⇒ **2018**

- o Facebook commits to forming a blockchain project and also raises the possibility of developing a cryptocurrency of its own.

- IBM is building a blockchain-based banking network with signing on to major banks like Citi and Barclays.

⇒ **2019**

- Bitcoin surpasses 400 million in total transactions.
- Facebook announces the cryptocurrency Libra
- Daily Ethereum transactions surpass one million

⇒ **2020**

- The Libra Association revamps its white paper and pulls back from its original vision.
- Singapore state-owned Temasek and San Francisco-based Paradigm and Slow Ventures join the Libra Association, bringing its total membership to 27.

Different Cryptocurrencies

Over 5000 cryptocurrencies are being traded with a total market capitalization of $201bn (as of 22 April 2020). A new cryptocurrency can be created at any time.

Below are some notable cryptocurrencies:

Year	Currency	Symbol	Founder(s)
2009	Bitcoin	BTC, XBT, ₿	Satoshi Nakamoto
2011	Litecoin	LTC, Ł	Charlie Lee
2011	Namecoin	NMC	Vincent Durham
2012	Peercoin	PPC	Sunny King (pseudonym)
2013	Dogecoin	DOGE, XDG, Ð	Jackson Palmer & Billy Markus
2013	Gridcoin	GRC	Rob Hälfordl
2013	Primecoin	XPM	Sunny King (pseudonym)
2013	Ripple	XRP	Chris Larsen & Jed McCaleb
2013	Nxt	NXT	BCNext (pseudonym)

Year	Currency	Symbol	Founder(s)
2014	Auroracoin	AUR	Baldur Odinsson (pseudonym)
2014	Dash	DASH	Evan Duffield & Kyle Hagan
2014	NEO	NEO	Da Hongfei & Erik Zhang
2014	MazaCoin	MZC	BTC Oyate Initiative
2014	Monero	XMR	Monero Core Team
2014	NEM	XEM	UtopianFuture (pseudonym)
2014	PotCoin	POT	Potcoin core dev team
2014	Titcoin	TIT	Edward Mansfield & Richard Allen
2014	Verge	XVG	Sunerok
2014	Stellar	XLM	Jed McCaleb
2014	Vertcoin	VTC	David Muller
2015	Ether or "Ethereum"	ETH	Vitalik Buterin
2015	Ethereum Classic	ETC	

Year	Currency	Symbol	Founder(s)
2015	Nano	Nano	Colin LeMahieu
2015	Tether	USDT	Jan Ludovicus van der Velde
2016	Zcash	ZEC	Zooko Wilcox
2017	Bitcoin Cash	BCH	
2017	EOS.IO	EOS	Dan Larimer
2018	Petro	PTR	Venezuelan Government
2019	Libra	LIBRA	Facebook

Digital Economy

Digital economy, often known as the Internet Economy, New Economy, or Online Economy, refers to an environment where digital computing technologies are used in economic activities.

It is the product of billions of daily online interactions between individuals, companies, computers, data, and processes. It is focused on the interconnectedness of individuals, organizations, and machines resulting from the Internet, mobile devices, and the Internet of Things (IoT).

The digital economy is driven by the introduction of Information and Communication Technologies (ICT) in all business sectors to increase productivity. Digital economic change threatens traditional conceptions of how businesses are organized, how customers get services, information, and products, and how states need to respond to these emerging regulatory challenges.

A Japanese professor and research economist first described the term 'Digital Economy' during the 1990s recession in Japan. The word followed in the west and was coined in Don Tapscott's book of 1995, "The Digital

Economy: Potential and Risk in the Era of Networked Intelligence."

It was one of the first books that discussed how the Internet might change the way we were doing business. The digital economy presents unique challenges for law enforcement. Decentralized currencies like Bitcoin and the anonymity associated with it, has led to its complete acceptance in illegal trade, particularly in the Dark Web. It pose challenges to efforts in combating money laundering and other illicit activities.

Illegal drugs, firearms, hacking tools, and toxic chemicals are all traded mostly using cryptocurrencies. On the other hand, the underlying technology behind these currencies (blockchain) will likely revolutionize finance by making transactions faster and more secure, regulatory frameworks need to ensure the financial integrity of the system and protect consumers while at the same time, support efficiency and innovation. What makes the digital currencies enticing also makes them potentially dangerous.

7 THE DARK SIDE

E very new technology or invention has both positive and negative impacts, like the two sides of a coin. The onion routing protocol has its objectives behind its discovery. Unfortunately, the onion services are used for implementing the Dark Web, which is notoriously famous for illegal activities.

Dark Web is estimated to process $500,000 in transactions per day. Users can buy fake passports for as little as $1,000. Bitcoin lottery cards, fake vouchers, and even counterfeit qualifications are all available for the right amount.

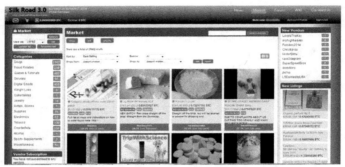

Fig: Silk Road Dark Site

The Dark Web is a tiny branch of the Deep Web that is mostly made up of all kinds of websites that market narcotics, guns and even employ assassins.

Silk Road was a famous Dark Net market known for selling illegal drugs, launched in 2011. However, it was closed down in 2014 by the Federal Bureau of Investigation (FBI).

IBM reported that an increasing number of cyberattacks come via the Tor network, largely in from the Dark Web. This report exposes new techniques where cyber-criminals use Tor hidden services for their ransomware campaigns. Transactions on the Dark Web have generally been by Bitcoin, which is untraceable. The sender or receiver does not need to know the identity of each other.

U.S. Immigration and
Customs Enforcement

THIS HIDDEN SITE HAS BEEN SEIZED

**as part of a joint law enforcement operation by
the Federal Bureau of Investigation, ICE Homeland Security Investigations,
and European law enforcement agencies acting through Europol and Eurojust**

in accordance with the law of European Union member states
and a protective order obtained by the United States Attorney's Office for the Southern District of New York
In coordination with the U.S. Department of Justice's Computer Crime & Intellectual Property Section
issued pursuant to 18 U.S.C. § 983(j) by the
United States District Court for the Southern District of New York

The Tor network can be used as a platform for terrorist funding. It is practically tough to monitor transactions for the growth, service, and propaganda of terrorists and associations, that mostly happen in cryptocurrencies like Bitcoin. Tor can help to conceal the user IP address in such instance, providing anonymity of bitcoin trades. It must be said that bitcoins can be bought by almost any Tor user for the US Dollar, Euro, or any other currencies. For example, a criminal might ask to send bitcoins into the bitcoin wallet address that doesn't include actual contact information or any traceability. The bitcoins can be converted into different fiat currencies deposited in an account.

Data leaked as part of the various data breaches over time are put for sale on the Dark Web. Data breaches frequently threaten consumer information. In the first six months of 2019 alone, 4.1 billion personal details were exposed due to data breaches. The guiding factor behind this is the competitive and sustainable environment that personal data finds on the Dark Web. After drugs, bank details and card details are the second most demanded commodity in the Dark Web.

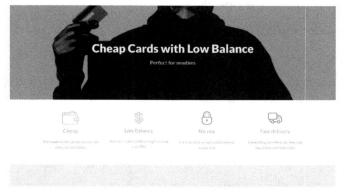

Fig: Carding Dark Site

Carding is one of the new and trending financial fraud in the cyberspace. It is also known as Credit Card Stuffing. Criminals use stolen card information to purchase goods from e-commerce sites or physical sellers. Then, they sell the products to someone else at a lower price, thereby liquidating the cash. Carding mainly focuses on the Dark Web, where anyone can buy the card details. The hackers dump millions of card information, which is stolen by various fraudulent activities.

One scenario is that few people feel the comfort of not leaving the seat for payments at restaurants. We sometimes give our cards to the staff for paying the bill, and for ease and support, we write down the pin on the bill and give it to them. They swipe the card and make the payment on behalf of us. When an individual receives the card number, expiry date, CVV, or PIN, he/she can make online transactions. For international online purchases, mostly PIN/OTP is not even required.

Banks have already introduced as an option for their customers to block/unblock their card transactions. The users get an opportunity to manage their ATM withdrawal, online transaction, and international transactions. The customers can unblock whenever they need and block it after use. Hence, users can ensure that the card is not misused. The feature is available in Internet Banking, Mobile banking, and even via SMS methods. Making use of these provisions can get rid of financial fraud to a certain extent.

8 APPLICATIONS

Because the Dark Web provides anonymity for its users, it is quite useful, particularly for whistle-blowers. Julian Assange's ever-famous WikiLeaks utilized Tor for the study and dissemination of massive repositories with encrypted or otherwise limited government documents concerning fighting terrorism and corruption.

To date, more than 10 million papers and relevant analyzes have been released. The Dark Web often decreases the possibility of government censorship that can be anticipated from the existence of WikiLeaks' material.

An open-source software platform, SecureDrop, used for secure communication between journalists and sources (whistle-blowers) uses Tor. SecureDrop utilizes Tor to enable interaction with whistle-blowers, journalists, and news agencies. SecureDrop sites are only available as secret facilities within the Tor network.

When a person visits the SecureDrop site, a randomly created code name is given. The code name is used to submit details to a particular author or publisher.

Fig: SecureDrop Implementation at The Guardian

Investigative journalists may use SecureDrop to reach the informant. As a consequence, the informant will take note of their random codeword.

Few other applications are:

1. **Gain Anonymity on Public Wi-Fi**: Employing open hotspots can be dangerous. Sending your information unencrypted through open hotspots, which are unknown, may cause a violation of privacy.

2. **Better Mobile Security**: Using Tor in an iOS or Android device adds an extra layer of security and anonymity to your data, so that, nobody can see who you are or where you are located, if sending info through mobile towers, or when traveling, Tor may lock your details.

3. **Break through Censorship Barriers**: If you are traveling through a nation or live in a country with strict online censorship legislation, you might need to use Tor. The Tor Browser anonymizes and encrypts traffic, enabling it to get to the free and open Internet. You won't need to think about censorship agencies monitoring your

data and will be able to view sites normally inaccessible in those areas.

4. **Anonymous Posting**: Tor is an ideal solution if you need to get some info published without revealing your identity.

5. **Reporting Corruption or Abuse**: Using Tor, you can submit corruption or abuse reports without attaching IP address or your own identity into the message.

This is particularly helpful when you may end up in legal issues for revealing information about your company or government.

6. **Internal Accountability in an organization**: In a transparent and healthy corporate environment, the staff should feel free to disclose any internal misconduct. Tor can implement this internal accountability. Onion routing protocol lets you share files of any size, securely and anonymously.

It is also possible to customize the features in a way that once the file is received at the receiving end, the sharing link is deactivated automatically, which prevents any further data leakage using the same link. (e.g., *Onion Share*)

Used by popular news media in acquiring sensitive content anonymously, at a corporate level, the feature can be used to share critical and sensitive data within and outside the company.

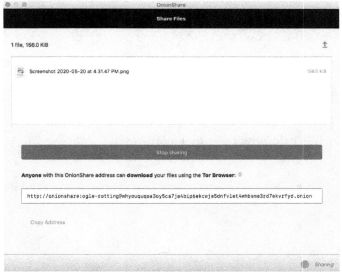

Fig: Onion Share

7. **Carry out Sensitive Business Activities**: Communicating using Tor ensures no leaks or no third parties watching over your shoulders, to an extent.

8. **Using Tor with a VPN**: Tor provides safety and anonymity, but it is not an end-all alternative for your privacy requirements. The main drawback is the inability

to utilize it effectively because of the lack of speed. Selecting the VPN to use with Tor is a matter of locating the service with the most privacy preferences.

Another application of Tor is in ZeroNet, which is a distributed network of peer-to-peer applications. Instead of an IP address, sites are defined by a cryptographic key. Sites can be viewed from a standard web browser by using the ZeroNet client, which serves as a local web host for that website. ZeroNet is anonymous and covers its IP address using the built-in Tor feature.

CONCLUSION

Tor has long been used by whistle-blowers, scholars, or thrill-seekers in highly censored countries to conceal their online surfing patterns and physical locations, browse around the Dark Web, and share details anonymously. More than 57% of the Dark Web is filled with illegal pornography, illicit banking, narcotics platform, arms distribution, counterfeit money streaming, and much more. The Dark Web is described as anything unlawful instead of a "Data Pool."

Tor is a champion in the realm of online privacy. Its browser supplies customers with the freedom to visit any website they like and offers them a certain degree of online anonymity. Tor is closely watched by law enforcement because criminals use the browser for carrying out their activities. The service is simple and completely free to download but does have its limitations. If you want to use the Tor browser, be cautious with unsafe pages and secure yourself against malware with adequate virus protection.

Using other security measures in conjunction with Tor could be an excellent strategy to protect yourself. The Tor browser can provide a fun, anonymous online experience for free.

ABOUT THE AUTHORS

Adarsh Nair is a thought leader in the field of Information

Security and Cyber Safety. His areas of expertise include Ethical Hacking, Information Security, and Compliance. He is a speaker at various national and international conferences and has published multiple articles on Ransomware, Financial Frauds, Phishing, Social Engineering Attacks, and Dark Web. Website: *https://adarshnair.com*

Greeshma M R is an entrepreneur, author, and freelance writer. She writes articles, poems, and is an online content creator. She has an educational background in Information Technology and Translational Engineering. Her interest areas include the Interaction of Technology & Humans,

Sustainable Development, Gender & Society. LinkedIn: *https://www.linkedin.com/in/greeshmamr*

♠ ♠ ♠